Sew Healthy & Happy

Smart Ergonomics, Stretches & More for Makers

Rose Parr

C&T PUBLISHING

Text and artwork copyright © 2021 by Rosalie Rennick-Parr
Photography copyright © 2021 by C&T Publishing, Inc.

Publisher: Amy Barrett-Daffin
Creative Director: Gailen Runge
Acquisitions Editor: Roxane Cerda
Managing Editor: Liz Aneloski
Editor: Beth Baumgartel
Technical Editor: Debbie Rodgers
Cover/Book Designer: April Mostek
Production Coordinator: Zinnia Heinzmann
Production Editor: Alice Mace Nakanishi
Illustrators: Noko Cloud and Alicia Georgie

Published by C&T Publishing, Inc., P.O. Box 1456, Lafayette, CA 94549

Library of Congress Cataloging-in-Publication Data
Names: Parr, Rose, 1963- author.
Title: Sew healthy & happy : smart ergonomics, stretches & more for makers / Rose Parr.
Other titles: Sew healthy and happy : smart ergonomics, stretches and more for makers
Description: Lafayette, CA : C&T Publishing, [2021] | Includes bibliographical references.
Identifiers: LCCN 2020037851 | ISBN 9781644030714 (trade paperback) | ISBN 9781644030721 (ebook)
Subjects: LCSH: Human engineering. | Work design. | Sewing. | Irons (Pressing) | Quilting. | Stretching exercises.
Classification: LCC TA166 .P367 2021 | DDC 646.2--dc23
LC record available at https://lccn.loc.gov/2020037851

Printed in China

10 9 8 7 6 5 4 3 2 1

Dedication

This book is for all you makers—whether you sew, crochet, knit, scrapbook, or do any crafting. In the following pages, discover what ergonomics can do for you and then create your pain-free workstations without breaking the bank. Next, look through the stretches and decide which ones you want to try first. Let's all sew, make, create, and quilt until we're 100!

Acknowledgments

A very special thank-you to the C&T Publishing team and to the quilters and wellness professionals who have generously shared their favorite tips and tricks:

Sarah Ashford, Jo Avery, Rosalie Brown, Jenna Clements, Jenny Doan, Brigitte Heitland, Krista Hennebury, Stuart Hillard, Tamara Kelly, Bernadette Kent, Isobel King, Melissa Marginet, Dr. Stuart McGill, Steve Nabity, Pat Skibinski, Kirsten Smith, Christa Watson, Suzy Williams

CONTENTS

ERGONOMICS   6

Ergonomics 101   6

Studio Design   8

CUTTING   14

Cutting 101: The Table   14

Rulers and Rotary Cutters   17

Cutting Technique   20

PRESSING   22

Pressing 101   22

Pain-Free Pressing Checklist   26

Seated Pressing   28

Look Up   29

SEWING   30

Sewing 101: Getting Set Up   30

Have a Seat   33

Sit/Stand Sewing Stations   35

A New Slant   37

Machine Quilting   38

Longarm Quilting   40

Handiwork   41

HEALTHY QUILTING: STRETCHING AND HEALTHY HABITS   43

Stretches for Quilters   45

Healthy Habits   65

Simple Smoothies   68

Quick, Nutrient-Dense Snacks with Rosalie Brown   69

Avocados, Good for the Body   70

Workshop Dos and Don'ts   72

THE PROS BEHIND THE TIPS   74

CREDITS/RESOURCES   79

ABOUT THE AUTHOR   80

ERGONOMICS

Ergonomics 101

Throughout my fifteen years as a certified personal trainer I've seen what bad habits can do to the most expensive piece of equipment in your sewing room—that would be you! The good news is that with a little "machine maintenance" and implementing simple ergonomic strategies, you can craft, sew, and quilt pain-free for years to come.

Ergonomics is the study of working comfortably and efficiently.

When I worked in corporate wellness, I saw firsthand how making small changes had a huge impact on employees' health and safety. Repetitive tasks both inside and outside the workplace cause residual strain and discomfort in our lives. Luckily for us, ergonomists have developed strategies to help people get things done without pain or injury.

Ergonomists Study Three Factors in the Workplace

These same three factors that are studied in the workplace—areas of concern, risk factors, and areas affected—translate directly to the sewing studio.

In other words, where, how, and how often you cut, press, and sew is essential in reducing any negative impact on your neck, shoulders, and wrists, to name a few hot spots.

Areas of Concern	Risk Factors	Areas Affected
• Cutting table	• Awkward positions	• The entire body (primarily the neck, shoulders, back and wrists) can all be affected by musculoskeletal disorders.
• Pressing station	• Action duration	
• Sewing area	• Action frequency	
	• Force applied	

" *Quilting should be fun! Enjoy the journey and remember that if you make a mistake it could just be a whole new pattern! My patterns are more like guidelines for creativity, rather than strict regulations.*" —Jenny Doan

Studio Design

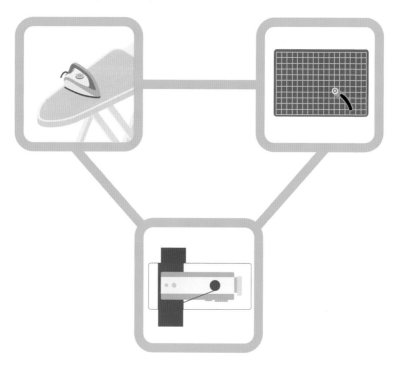

A "work triangle" is the key to designing your sewing area. The stove, sink, and refrigerator placement are a time-tested work triangle found in every home and industrial kitchen. The goal is to eliminate wasted effort and time by keeping the three primary work zones close.

In a kitchen, architects suggest that no side of the triangle be less than 4 feet or more than 9 feet. However, when setting up your sewing area, aim for bigger distances between workstations. If your sewing room is small, set your ironing board up in another room to get you up and moving. Bonus points for putting it on a different floor! This might not seem efficient to you, and you would be right because I am suggesting an "inefficient" sewing studio. Inefficient does *not* mean ineffective.

One strategy to prevent discomfort, fatigue, and injury is to vary your current activity to allow working muscles, joints, and tissues time to rest and recover. Muscles that remain in the same position tire faster, and circulation decreases, leading to discomfort.

This may mean taking a minute to focus on a different task, rest your eyes, and most of all, change position. Prolonged sitting is one of the major risk factors for lower back pain, so give your back a break and stand, walk, and stretch. It may also mean switching to a task that uses different muscle groups and postures. If you have 60 half-square triangles to sew, chain piece 20 or 30, then get up and press them.

While our work triangle may appear inefficient, we want our muscles to work as effectively as possible. For example, store heavier items at waist height so you don't have to bend or reach to retrieve them. Efficient use of your muscles exerts as little force as possible while accomplishing the most work and reduces the chance of injury.

" *Place your ironing board on the other side of the room relative to your sewing machine to make sure you get up and move around regularly. Long spells of inactivity are not good for you.*" —Jo Avery

In 1928, Lillian Gilbreth developed the work triangle, still used by architects today. She also patented designs for the shelves in your refrigerator doors and the foot-pedal trash can. You may know her as the real *Cheaper by the Dozen* mom. Look her up!

Lighting

Poor lighting can cause headaches, eyestrain, brain fog, inability to see colors correctly, and tiredness. Reduce eye strain by using "cheater" eyeglasses, magnified lighting, and by improving your overall lighting. Good overhead lighting is important not only for practical purposes but also for your mood. If the ceiling fixture isn't ideal, install brighter bulbs and consider removing the fixture's cover, or hang additional plug-in lighting.

Task lighting is key to reducing eyestrain and for better color visibility.

• Position floor lamps over your sewing and cutting tables and your favorite sewing chair.

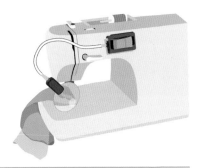

• Consider specialized task lighting over your machine's needle so you don't have to lean in to see better.

• Try a light with built-in magnification for hand stitching.

- Optimally, all lighting should be combined with natural lighting, which helps you see colors better when pulling fabrics for your next project. The more sunlight we are exposed to, the better we feel.

Full-spectrum lighting signals your body to regulate alertness, sleep cycles, and mood. The flip side is that by overexposing your eyes to high levels of full-spectrum light or blue screen light, the production of melatonin is suppressed. With the sunset, your body produces higher levels of melatonin, which is a natural signal that it's time to start thinking about sleep; but melatonin production can be hindered when bright indoor lighting and electronic screens illuminate the world at night.

> **Use the "20-20-20 rule." Every 20 MINUTES take a 20-SECOND BREAK and focus your eyes on something at least 20 FEET AWAY.**

" *Early evenings are perfect for cozying up with crochet and knitting projects—but you need a good light to stitch by. When you see better, you craft better!"* —**Tamara Kelly**

" *If you're struggling to see where you've quilted, turn out the lights! At the very least turn them down ... harsh artificial lighting can make seeing quilting really hard ... natural light is better and will help you to see where you've been and where you're going!"* —**Stuart Hillard**

Anti-Fatigue Mats

All anti-fatigue mats are not created equal. The highest-quality mats are designed for standing all day in steel-toe shoes in factories, garages, and industrial kitchens. While you may not require an industrial-grade mat, it's still important to use a mat that is thick enough to withstand daily pounding without breaking down. The best anti-fatigue mats maintain their buoyancy, just like your shoes, so they don't lose their cushioning over time. Choose a mat that provides cushioning but is not so soft that you wobble or cannot stand on it comfortably.

CONSIDERATIONS WHEN PURCHASING A MAT

THICKNESS   Good mats for sewing should be at least ⅝″ thick, and better ones will be ¾″ thick. Mats that are ¼″ or ⅜″ thick provide little relief.

COMPRESSION MATERIAL   Compression mats are made from various sources including rubber, foam, and gel. Gel and foam mats offer more cushioning, but also compress faster. This means the user needs to move on and off the mat to allow it to decompress, which you are doing when moving between your workstations. If a mat is too soft, it will "bottom out" under your weight and become as hard as the floor. You only want enough cushioning to encourage your body to shift and rebalance.

UNDERSIDE GRIP   Your mat should have enough underside grip so that it stays put, but not be so sticky that you can't reposition it easily.

EDGE STYLE   Sloped or beveled edges provide a gradual transition to the floor and minimizes tripping hazards.

SEAM STYLE   Durable mats with no visible seams prevent spilled water from absorbing into the mat.

> *An anti-fatigue mat basically does what sneakers do—gives your feet cushioning and support. I really like the added energy and the way I feel after a day of standing compared to a day of sitting, so I'll deal with an ugly mat."* —Suzy Williams

Cutting 101: The Table

The magic angle for efficient and comfortable (ergonomic) work is between 90° and 110°. The 90° angle formed by bending your elbow provides the least amount of strain on the wrist and shoulder when cutting a pattern with scissors. However, with rotary cutters it's a little different; the best angle is closer to 110°.

A rotary cutter requires the application of force, which is why a sharp blade is so important. The sharper the blade, the less force you need to exert. It's best to use gravity and apply this force from above.

Measuring for the Perfect-Height Cutting Table

Even two people of the same height can have different arm and leg lengths, so measure to be sure. Follow these steps to determine your perfect-height table for cutting with scissors or with a rotary cutter.

1. Stand with your hips square and both feet facing the table.

2. Relax your shoulders and let your arms hang at your sides, keeping your elbows close to your side.

3. Keeping the top half of your arm at your side, bring your right hand up with your palm down, creating a 90° bend at your elbow.

4. Have a friend measure from the floor to your hand. If no one is nearby, hold a measuring tape with your other hand and step on it where it meets the floor. This is your baseline measurement; 1″–2″ below this works well if you primarily work with scissors.

5. *For rotary blade cutting:* Allow your arm to naturally fall 3″–6″, keeping your wrist neutral-straight and shoulder down. Don't bend your wrist and let your hand droop; we want a straight line from your elbow to the rotary cutter. Measure again to determine the ideal table height for rotary cutting (typically 3″–4″ shorter than the baseline measurement).

> " *Make a quick and easy lightbox to help with tracing. Take a small shallow cardboard box with no lid and pop your phone inside it with the torch or flashlight function switched on. Place a large square patchwork ruler on the box and trace your pattern on top of this."* —Jo Avery

I am 5´3˝ in shoes and my 90° elbow bend is 39˝. I subtract 4˝ from 39˝ for a table height of 35˝ for rotary cutting.

Customizing Your Cutting Station

There are several ways to bring your cutting surface up to snuff. Your choice depends on your current table, skill set and available tools, budget, and personal preference.

FOR A FOLDING TABLE WITH METAL LEGS, add height with PVC piping.

1. Measure from the knuckle/bend of one leg to the tabletop's underside; next, measure the thickness of the table. Add these numbers together and deduct this sum from the ideal table height.

2. Determine the size of PVC pipe that will fit over the lower leg. Cut 4 pieces all the length calculated in Step 1. Be generous, you can always shave some off. Measure twice, cut once.

IF YOU ARE LUCKY ENOUGH TO HAVE A WOODEN TABLE, you can purchase ready-made table legs in a variety of sizes to increase its existing height.

BED RISERS ARE A FAST, INEXPENSIVE WAY TO RAISE ANY TABLE. Standard sizes are 3″, 5″, and 6″. They fit any table leg but work better on wooden table legs. It is easy to bump a table with smaller diameter metal legs off the risers, so do be careful.

" Avoid thread 'bird's nests' and chewed fabric when machine piecing by holding the top and bobbin thread in your left hand and pulling gently backwards as you take the first few stitches. Helping to guide your fabric through the feed dogs on those first couple of stitches eliminates any issues!" —**Stuart Hillard**

Rulers and Rotary Cutters

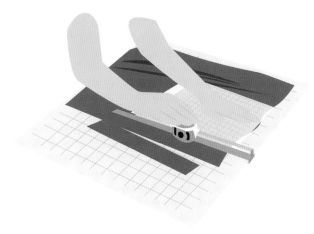

Years ago, I decided that running was not for me. My joints were not happy with the pounding and the pain, so I decided to save my hips and knees and have enjoyed hiking and walking ever since. That's how you should look at your cutting tools. You can't change your genetics, but you can make decisions to save your joints when you can. It all adds up!

Cutting tools that combine a blade and ruler in one are a great way to save your hands. If you have lost grip strength, these cutting tools can keep you sewing longer. If you cut fabric with scissors, try bent-handle shears with molded handles for comfort and better grip.

The following tools are handy additions to your cutting station.

PREPACKAGED RUBBER PIECES applied to the underside of your ruler provide a good grip, so you don't have to work as hard to keep it in place. Tape from your first-aid kit works as well.

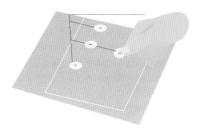

" The number of layers you can cut is determined by the thickness and type of fabric, always begin with fewer layers and build up. For scrappy quilts, layer up to 6 different fabrics together and cut, great stash buster." —Steve Nabity

RULER GRIPS, to hold the ruler in place, have large comfortable handles that make them ideal for weak or arthritic hands. The suction cups can be locked and easily released to reposition. They also keep your fingers safe from the blade of the rotary cutter.

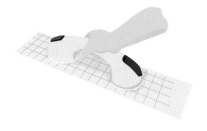

ERGONOMIC ROTARY CUTTERS are designed to reduce the pressure in your wrist and fingers and distribute it evenly across your arm, wrist, and hand. Some brands use less downward pressure, which means the cutting table can be slightly higher.

Change your blade! #rotarycutterbattlescars

"Geometric dies have specially designed dog-eared corners and ¼" seam allowances to save trimming time. The blades on some die designs are positioned at an angle to the board, to get the most accurate cut, align fabric to the edge of the die blade, not the edge of the board."

"Die blades are designed for repetitive cutting and never need to be sharpened. Extend the life of your mat by alternating the sides when cutting. Use a die pick or tweezers to remove scraps of fabric from tight areas between die blades and a lint roller to remove lint and tiny scraps from the foam side of die." —**Steve Nabity**

SEW HEALTHY & HAPPY

FABRIC CUTTING SYSTEMS are accurate, cut multiple layers, and minimize the strain on your hands and wrists. On days that you need a break, use your cutter for your bindings and borders. It's magic!

Here are few tips from Steve Nabity, the inventor of the AccuQuilt cutting system:

- For perfect half-square triangles, layer fabric on die with right sides together, and then cut. Pick up one pair from the pile and sew. (Brilliant!)

- Apply fusible web before die cutting for fast appliqué.

- For accuracy, cut on the lengthwise grain as the fabric goes under the roller. This is particularly important when cutting geometric shapes.

"To get the straightest cuts, stand squarely in front of your table and cutting mat. Imagine that your cutting arm is against a wall, and cut straight out from your body, imagining that your shoulder, elbow, and wrist are all in contact with the wall beside you." —**Krista Hennebury**

To reduce strain on your wrist, arms, and back, make sure your cutting table is the correct height, stand up straight and squarely in front of your table and cutting mat, and steady your ruler with a slightly tented hand.

Wrist-friendly technique

" One of my favorite tricks is to use specialty rulers for any tasks that require accuracy. So, for example, I like the Bloc Loc Rulers for any half-square triangles, half-rectangle triangles, and curved seams, like drunkard's path." —**Brigitte Heitland**

" When free-cutting without a ruler, protect your non-cutting hand by putting it on your hip or in your pocket. If you must stabilize your fabric, be very aware of the path you plan to take with your rotary cutter." —**Krista Hennebury**

Familiar technique

When you press down on your ruler with full force, willing it not to budge, your wrist pays the price! This can disturb the blood flow to your hand. Whenever your circulation is disrupted, you increase your chance of repetitive strain injuries.

FOR A JOINT-FRIENDLY TECHNIQUE, TRY THESE TIPS:

• Tent your fingers (think of yoga toes) to disperse the force to five pressure points instead of to just one spot on your wrist.

• Keep your wrist in a neutral-straight position.

• Center your body over your work.

• Anchor your ruler from below for better grip and to prevent it from sliding. See Rulers and Rotary Cutters (page 17).

PRESSING

Pressing 101

There are two very common pressing mistakes: having your ironing board too high, which forces an awkward wrist position, and having it set too low.

At first glance, the lady in blue looks to be set up correctly.

Look closer at her hand; the bend in the wrist is almost imperceptible, but it's there. Your hand should be flat on top of your iron, with no bend in the wrist, with your forearm extending 1″–2″ below your elbow. In order to hold the iron correctly, the ironing board needs to be set to the correct height.

The average pain-free ironing height is approximately 1″–2″ below your hip bone. Ironing boards have a limited number of adjustment choices and the one in the illustration is just a bit too high. Going an inch lower is better than higher if you can maintain good posture.

Having your board too low not only affects your neck and back, but since the work is farther away, your eyes feel the strain as well. You do need to see what you're doing from time to time and you will need to look down; however, setting the ironing board to the correct height will help your back, wrist, and eyes.

" Press (don't push) your iron along the seam rather than across it, so it doesn't bow and look like a rainbow." —**Stuart Hillard**

Customizing Your Ironing Board

There are several things you can do to make pressing painless.

Make sure the ironing board is high enough to prevent you from bending over but low enough that your wrist doesn't hook over the top of your iron. Stand tall without over-correcting, which may result in what is known as a swayback. If you do lean toward a swayback, try placing a small footstool directly in front of your left foot (if you are right-handed, and vice versa if you are left-handed) to keep your hips level.

Place your ironing board away from your sewing machine so you get up and move every time you use it. If you are sewing in a tight space, a foldable tabletop ironing board can add the height you need. Keep it a few steps away from your sewing machine so you have to get up to use it.

Calculating Your Perfect Ironing Board Height

Stand facing your board *wearing your indoor shoes*. Bend your elbow to 90°. Measure from your elbow to the floor. Your most pain-free pressing happens when your elbow is between a 90° and 110° angle and your hand is on top of your iron—*not* the ironing board. If you measure to the top of the board, your wrist will have to bend to hold the iron. This disrupts circulation to the hand and may lead to repetitive stress/strain injuries to your wrist and tension in your shoulders.

Measure your iron from the plate to the top of the handle, this is usually between 5″–6″.

SO, HERE'S THE CALCULATION:

Distance from floor to elbow
– Iron height
= *Pain-free pressing*
   ironing board height

I'm 5′3″ in shoes.

Bent elbow to floor = 39″

Iron height = 6″

Ironing board height = 33″

Pain-Free Pressing Checklist

- Make sure your ironing board is set at the correct height.

- Maintain a neutral stance with your weight centered, body relaxed, spine in natural slight S-curve.

- Center your body on the iron; irons are heavy, so keep it as close to you as safety allows.

- Your elbow is bent at approximately 90°–110°.

- Your hand should be flat on top of your iron, with no bend in the wrist, 1″–2″ below your elbow.

- Stand with your shoulders set and chest out.

  Why set your shoulders? Roll your shoulders back, naturally drawing the shoulder blades together. An expanded chest allows us to breathe deeply, pumping oxygenated blood through the body, providing energy for more sewing time. It also opens the heart chakra, and who doesn't want more love, forgiveness, and compassion in their world?

- Distribute your weight evenly on both feet.

  Why distribute your weight? Prolonged standing and bearing more weight on one leg causes imbalances in the lower body, resulting in pain and eventually limiting daily activities. (If you held a baby on your hip, you know the pain I'm referring to.) Be sure to move and shift your weight (dancing is good!); but when standing still, keep your weight balanced.

- Look forward and whenever possible Look Up (page 29).

> "*Press to the dark side to hide seams.*" —Jenny Doan

PRESSING

27

Seated Pressing

If you have a big stack of blocks to press, have a seat. Whether you have a stool that works for the regular height of your ironing board or you lower the board so you can use a chair, the basic guidelines apply. This is a great way to catch up on your favorite shows and the television will prompt you to look up.

- Elbows between 90° and 110° (to the top of the iron—*not* the ironing board)

- Feet flat on the floor (or on a stool) to distribute weight

- No slouching

" *Whenever I do chain piecing, or any other kind of routine tasks, I like listening to an entertaining audio book. I enjoy the combination of doing my hand craft work and having a good story to go along with it".*
—**Brigitte Heitland**

" *When removing the paper backing from fusible appliqué shapes, scratch an X into the paper with a pin and tear the paper out toward the edges. Quick, easy, and no distorted or frayed edges!"*
—**Stuart Hillard**

Look Up

Where the eyes go, the neck follows. You spend so much time looking down that it helps to have cues to remind yourself to look up. Positioning your sewing station near a window improves your mood, provides good lighting, and helps strengthen your eye muscles when you look in the distance. Fill your studio with beautiful things and place them up high.

Anything that prompts you to look up is a good thing. If you watch a laptop while working, get a wire rack used for stacking dishes and set your laptop on it, this will raise it 6″, which sets the screen nearer to eye level. A wall shelf, about 15″–20″ higher than your desk, is the perfect spot for your tablet. Place it where you won't be craning your neck to see it. Bulletin boards, family photos, textile art, orphan blocks, and motivational quotes are perfect for your creative space; they will help draw your eyes up and away from the sewing machine and bring you joy.

> " Take photos for social media in good light and use photo editing software to enhance them." —**Sarah Ashford**

Sewing 101: Getting Set Up

Ready

There is no such thing as one perfect sitting position, but there is such a thing as good posture and the correct height sewing surface. While seated, measure from the bottom of your elbow to the floor to determine how high your sewing surface should be. If your sewing machine is too high, you have to raise your elbows, which forces your shoulders to scrunch up and your wrists to bend, causing back, neck, and wrist pain. You probably need to either lower the table (dropping the machine as well) or raise your chair until your hands are resting on the sewing surface with your elbows at 90°–110°. If your feet are dangling, place a box under the sewing table until your feet are resting flat and your knees are at a 90°–110° angle. The pedal should be directly under your foot.

Center your body in front of the sewing machine needle, sit tall with a neutral, natural S-shaped spine, and relax your shoulders. Keep your upper arms at your sides and bend your elbows to 90°. Now all you need is a suitable chair.

Set

Choose a chair, using the information in Have a Seat (next page). Think about how you sit when you are sewing. Position your hips all the way back in the seat with your feet flat on the floor. Run your hand behind your knees, there shouldn't be any pressure on the front edge of the chair and your thighs should be parallel to the floor. Maintain a neutral spine and use lumbar support if needed.

Sew

As you get in the zone, chain piecing one block after another, your shoulders tend to roll forward, your head leans in so you can see better, your neck is bent, and back is hunched. Not great! Instead, sit tall, roll your shoulders back, slide them down your back, drawing your shoulder blades together—don't squeeze or tense up. Relax your shoulders, don't scrunch them up. When you stitch, use one foot for a bit, then move the pedal over and switch feet; this is good for your brain too.

" *Never prewash your precuts. They will end up a frayed mess! Fabrics have improved in quality so much that we don't need to worry about shrinkage or fading like we used to.*" —**Jenny Doan**

Have a Seat

What happens when you unbox your new machine or inherit one from a friend? You set it on a spare desk or table and pull up the nearest chair and start sewing! Yippee! Later you notice that your neck, shoulders, wrists, and back are sore. The problem is that the chair is designed for the user to work at the table—*not* 4″ above it. The average sewing machine is 3½″ from bottom to sewing surface.

You wouldn't drive a car without adjusting the seat, so why sit at your sewing machine without adjusting it to your specifications? Take the time to find the best seat in the house.

LOOK FOR A CHAIR THAT ...

... allows you to adjust the height. If you can't lower your table, you can raise your chair. If you can't adjust your chair, you can always add an extra cushion.

... has an adjustable back that provides lumbar support and an adjustable seat base depth. A cushion can also help here. Ideally, you should be able to tilt back when not sewing to redistribute weight on your pressure points; if you can't tilt, then wiggle, shift, or get up.

... has a waterfall edge at the front to eliminate pressure on the back of the knees which disrupts blood flow and circulation. Allow for a two- or three-finger gap from the front of the chair to the back of the knees.

"*Folding chairs are often too low for the banquet tables used at workshops. Try stacking two chairs or bring a firm cushion to sit on.*"
—**Krista Hennebury**

... has adjustable armrests, which you should position just below your elbows to prevent your shoulders from scrunching up. However, no armrests are better than the wrong armrests.

"*My best tip for successful machine quilting is to give yourself lots of practice time. Many people expect their quilting to be perfect right off the bat and don't realize that developing 'quilting penmanship' takes time.*" —**Christa Watson**

Sit/Stand Sewing Stations

Sitting is the new smoking, and quilters sit a lot. Standing, on the other hand puts your spine in a neutral position and strengthens your back muscles. In addition, you move around more as the shift from standing to walking is more natural than the shift from sitting to standing. While it's often not recommended to stand (still) for long periods at work, sewing is different since you use your foot pedal, guide fabric, and move to your ironing board. And, of course, you will be stretching! See Stretches for Quilters (page 45). A standing sewing station is not an outright replacement for sitting, but it is a great option. Switching between your regular table and a hydraulic, adjustable table is ideal. Sew standing for an hour and then either switch to another task or sew in a seated position for a while. Over time, increase your standing time and decrease the time you spend sitting and be sure to use an anti-fatigue mat!

Standing industrial sewing machine tables are often tilted 10°. Try raising your table's back legs; just make sure your machine is secure.

Another option is an in-between table set up using an ergonomic saddled stool like many hairstylists use. However, since many of these stools don't have back support, switch throughout the day. Regardless how long you stand to sew, take time to set things up right. It all adds up!

> " When I'm thinking, planning, or just taking a break, I like to stand on a balance board. It works my core muscles ever so slightly". —**Suzy Williams**

A New Slant

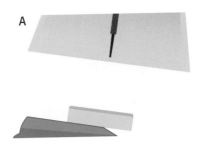

You may find that tilting your machine toward you (approximately 10°–15°, like a drafting table), reduces the amount you need to lean in to see and works especially well if you wear bi/trifocals. Your back will be straighter, reducing the strain on the back, neck, and wrists. There are adjustable models with a front ledge to keep your machine from sliding. You can also try a pair of wedge door stoppers (A), a laptop support, or a binder to raise the back of your machine (B). Quilters say tilting doesn't affect their computerized machines; I can't say whether it will or will not.

Your car's foot pedals don't move and neither should the one under your sewing machine. When you chase after it your previous perfect posture slips away. Your hips are misaligned, and the rest of your body is compensating.

Anchor your pedal with a rubber pad (C), sew one from an online tutorial, or try the quick fix from my blog (page 80).

> " Keep a set of rubber door stops in your travel case for workshops and retreats. If your setup isn't perfect, they might help with machine positioning." —**Krista Hennebury**

SEWING

37

Machine Quilting

Enjoying machine quilting *and* free-motion quilting (FMQ) begins with the basics of sewing ergonomics, good lighting, and chair selection as previously discussed. However, there are three more important considerations: the flow, bulk, and grip of the fabric.

FMQ is all about the flow and movement of your quilt across your work surface. The larger and smoother your surface is, the less drag you experience and the easier it is to stitch. A slider mat helps; just be sure you have it positioned properly so you don't stitch it into your quilt.

Anything bigger than a baby quilt can feel bulky in your machine. There are hanging systems that help you hang your quilt to reduce weight and there are clips to corral big quilts.

Moving your quilt around can be exhausting. The grip of gardening or quilting gloves reduces shoulder strain and makes it easier to hold onto the folded up sides of your project. You might want to consider the frames/hoops designed for FMQ, but as with any new tool, it's always nice to try before you buy.

" Use a large drop-in table for your sewing machine. If you can, add an extra small table to the left of your setup, forming an L. This will catch the weight of the quilt as you work. When you eliminate friction and drag on the quilt, the whole process becomes much more enjoyable!" —Christa Watson

" When quilting, have fun and don't stress. No one will notice if you're off, and if they do, they are looking too closely."
—Melissa Marginet

Longarm Quilting

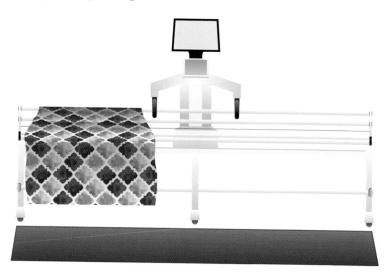

There isn't one single height that fits all the different things you do with your longarm machine, but there are ways to minimize daily strain. Experiment. Don't assume your first setup is the best setup.

- Stand in a neutral position, shoulders down, hips even, weight evenly distributed on both legs.

- Keep your wrists neutral, straight without bending them; adjust the handles accordingly.

- Grip the handles lightly; squeezing tires your hands.

- Use a raised chair for micro-work.

- For pantographs, raise your machine until you can guide the handles without leaning in and straining your lower back.

- When you work at the front of your machine, experiment with various heights for comfortable quilting.

- Place the front roller (belly bar) at your belly button or 2″–3″ below.

- Ruler lovers may prefer the front roller positioned under chest height so they can see further behind the needle; castors or wooden blocks can be used to raise the machine.

- For digital work, try positioning your roller at your 90° elbow or 3″ below. If your tablet is mounted above, it helps to have the frame lower to avoid craning to see the screen. A bar stool helps here as well; sit when you can.

- According to the pros at Handi Quilter, "Stand at the machine and look at the needle. Move the machine forward and backward and evaluate whether you can see the needle area clearly without bending left or right to see. Adjust the height until your sight path stays clear."

> " *For instantly better control when hand-guiding your longarm, try tucking your elbows in! Most of us naturally stick out our elbows when we grasp the handles. I call them our 'chicken wings.' Instead, tuck your elbows down against your sides for smoother, more accurate quilting.*" —**Stuart Hillard**

Handiwork

Your head weighs about 12 pounds, and for every inch that it is held forward in poor posture, an additional 10 pounds are felt on the cervical spine. Just 1˝ or 2˝ of bending forward to see your work can double or triple the load on your neck. Try raising your work.

To strengthen your neck muscles, tuck in your chin and press your head back into your car's headrest at every red light and hold until the light turns green.

When you lean in to work on your embroidery or other hand stitching, it's easy to bend your neck. Add to that the time spent on your phone or laptop and you've got a recipe for "text neck." Instead of bringing your head down to your work, bring your work up to your eyes. There are products available, such as the Lapp App, that hold your work to bring it closer to your eyes, allowing you to rest your arms as well.

You can also use magnified lighting or dollar-store reading glasses to bring work closer.

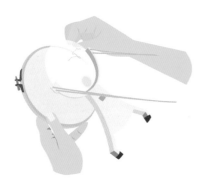

" When accidentally getting blood on your quilt when hand stitching, the perfect compound to remove the blood is your own saliva. In other words, spit on it, rub it, and continue until it disappears." —**Isobel King**

" When hand sewing on the sofa make sure to put a pillow (or two) on your lap to raise your work higher, try not to stoop down to your sewing or you can have shoulder problems later in life."

" Using a fine thread such as Aurifil 80-weight for the appliqué alongside a fine needle such as a straw milliners number 10 will help your stitches disappear." —**Jo Avery**

HEALTHY QUILTING:

Stretching and Healthy Habits

What makes a healthy person? My naturopath recently ordered me "to go to bed on the same day in which you wake up." She feels that it is not healthy to sew until 3 a.m., no matter how much you get done, but she is not a quilter. *Eat—Sleep—Move* might be good for the average soul, but for sewcialites it's *Eat—Sleep—Move—Sew*. The problem is that many quilters forget to eat, think that sleep is a waste of time, and never get up and move away from their sewing machine.

" *Have you ever focused so much on a project that you lost track of time? And neglected yourself in other ways? An Indian proverb reminds us to refocus on self and our health:*

'Everyone is a house
with four rooms:
a physical,
a mental,
an emotional,
and a spiritual.
Most of us tend to live in one room most of the time, but unless we go into every room every day, even if only to keep it aired, we are not a complete person.' " —Pat Skibinski

Edith Choiniere's House #3
"Amsterdam on the Canal"

Disclaimer: Consult your doctor or healthcare provider before starting any exercise program or trying any of the stretches or exercises on the following pages, especially if you have any injury, disease, disability, or other concerns. Some conditions can be worsened by exercise. If you experience any pain or difficulty with any exercise, stop immediately. Start slowly and do not push yourself too far or too fast. Listen to your body; pain is your body's way of telling you to stop and rest. Always warm up before stretching. Shake your fingers, rotate your ankles and wrists, roll your shoulders, or just walk around the room.

Stretches for Quilters

The stretches on the following pages are designed for any crafter to do anywhere. No need to get down on the floor or change into your exercise clothing.

Try to work stretching into every part of your day, while waiting for the bobbin to fill or the teakettle to boil. Refer to the drawing to determine what part of your body would benefit from a good stretch.

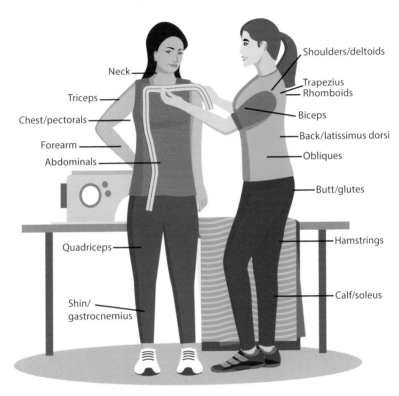

Neck

Triceps

Chest/pectorals

Forearm

Abdominals

Quadriceps

Shin/gastrocnemius

Shoulders/deltoids

Trapezius
Rhomboids

Biceps

Back/latissimus dorsi

Obliques

Butt/glutes

Hamstrings

Calf/soleus

" *Only exercise on the days you want to be in a better mood, feel more energetic, more confident, more clear-headed, more creative, more patient, and stronger. Other than that ... you can probably skip it.*" —Rosalie Brown

Getting Started

Why?

• Improves your flexibility and range of motion

• Makes daily activities easier

• Decreases risk of injuries

• Increases blood flow to your muscles

How?

• Unless otherwise noted, hold each stretch for 30–60 seconds, rest, and repeat.

• Always warm up. Shake your fingers, rotate your ankles and wrists, roll your shoulders, or just walk around the room.

• Don't bounce during or jerk out of your stretch.

• You should some feel tension, but not pain. If it hurts, stop—you've gone too far. Keep things even; stretch both sides even if one side isn't feeling tight.

• Warm up. Think of your muscles like a rubber band: If they're cold and dry, they're going to snap; if they are warm, they will stretch!

When?

• Your bobbin is reloading

• Your iron is reheating

• You're planning your next move

• Anytime you need a break

Where?

• Everywhere!

Share #stitchandstretch—post a picture of you stretching while loading your bobbin or waiting for your iron to warm up! Tag me @healthyquilting so I can see and share!

Allover Stretch

This stretches your forearms, shoulders, and torso and reenergizes your entire body.

1. Plant your feet squarely on the ground and sit up straight with an invisible thread drawing you up.

2. Move to the edge of the chair until your feet touch the floor.

3. As you extend your arms in front, interlace your fingers and turn your hands so that their backs face you.

4. Raise your arms overhead; stop when your arms are fully extended. Don't push beyond your shoulders' comfort level.

5. Hold for 30 seconds.

> " *Keep the floor and surface areas around your quilting space spotlessly clean. Quilts are a magnet for thread waste, which can end up stitched into your precious quilt.*" —**Stuart Hillard**

Neck and Shoulders

UPPER TRAPEZIUS STRETCH

While seated, grab the underside of your chair with one hand and gently lean your head to the opposite side to feel the stretch. Hold for 20 seconds. Then switch and repeat on the other side.

ASSISTED UPPER TRAPEZIUS

Place your opposite hand firmly on the shoulder of the side you need to stretch. The weight of your head will deepen the stretch more than just tilting your head to the side. Repeat for the other side.

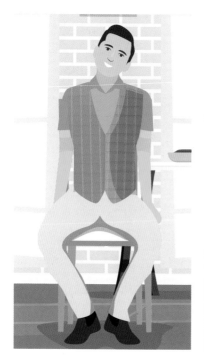

" Aging has its downsides as well as its perks. Society tends to create expectations that can limit us in enjoying our maturity. Live your life, not your age!" —**Pat Skibinski**

Hands

Flexing your fingers creates heat and stimulates the production of synovial fluid in joints, keeping them limber. Flexing can strengthen your hands and fingers and help relieve pain.

THUMB BENDS

Bend thumb toward palm, over to pinky or wherever you can; hold rest, repeat.

MAKE A FIST

Start with fingers straight, make soft fist, thumb on outside of hand. Release and spread fingers wide.

DIGIT BENDS

Move each finger slowly to meet your thumb; hold, straighten, and move on to next one.

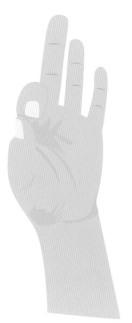

FINGER LIFT

Also known as *finger press*. With palm flat on table, fingers spread, lift each slowly off table; return each finger before raising next.

" *Working with fabric and yarn can be very drying; keep your hands well moisturized.*"
—**Kirsten Smith**

THE CLAW

Hold hand with palm facing you. Bend fingertips in to touch pads of hand, turning hand into claw shape. Hold 30 seconds; release.

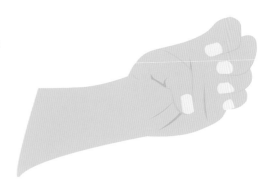

PINCH IT

Squeezing a ball strengthens grip, but pinching it between fingertips strengthens them and makes threading a needle easier. Hold 30 seconds; release.

" *Wear quilting gloves when quilting on your domestic machine to avoid strain on your hands.*" —**Melissa Marginet**

SEW HEALTHY & HAPPY

Forearms

WRIST AND FOREARM FLEXOR STRETCH

Stretching your forearms can alleviate tight muscles and may prevent the progression of carpal tunnel syndrome.

1. Sit or stand comfortably. Extend one arm in front, slightly below shoulder height.

2. Keeping your arm straight, bend your wrist, pointing your fingers upward. Think *stop sign*.

3. With the opposite hand, gently pull fingers toward you; hold for 10–20 seconds.

4. Straighten wrist, relax fingers, rest, and repeat on opposite forearm.

WRIST AND FOREARM EXTENSOR ENERGIZER

1. With your arms extended, make a fist with both hands.

2. Bend your wrists downward and hold for 10–20 seconds.

3. Relax fist and straighten wrists, wiggle fingers, rest, and repeat.

> " *Attending workshops or joining a local quilt group will help you to get the most out of patchwork and quilting. There is nothing more valuable than the encouragement and experience of others when you're learning a new skill."* —Jenna Clements

Triceps

1. Stand tall with your core engaged and your feet hip-width apart.

2. Roll your shoulders down and back.

3. Reach your right arm to the ceiling.

4. Bending at the elbow, let your right hand drop between your shoulder blades, as if you are trying to scratch your back.

5. Reach your left hand up toward the ceiling and place your left fingers on your right elbow; apply light pressure to deepen the stretch; don't forget to breathe.

6. Hold for 20–40 seconds, rest, and repeat on opposite side.

Try adding a side stretch, bending away from stretched arm.

> " *Use a bobbin thread that matches your background, this will allow you to have a great-looking stitch even if your tension is not perfect. Never pull the thread backward out of your machine, snip at the spool and at the eye of the needle, then pull the thread toward the needle; your machine will thank you.*" —**Bernadette Kent**

Lower Back Release

1. Sit at the edge of your chair, and place your hands on the chair seat behind you or on your lower back, whichever is more comfortable for your wrists.

2. Prop yourself up, drawing your chest up to lift your lower back.

3. Lengthen your spine; slowly arch your back and gently tilt your head and look up.

4. Hold, release, rest, and repeat.

Standing Row

Strengthen your back to improve your posture.

1. Anchor a resistance band around a door handle or another heavy stationary object at approximately waist height.

2. Stand 2–3 feet back, holding the ends of the resistance band.

3. Roll your shoulders back; keep your chest up, and your eyes looking straight ahead.

4. Brace your core, draw in your shoulder blades, with your arms in front and your palms facing each other.

5. Draw your elbows back and down, skimming them past the sides of your body; your upper and lower arms should form a 90° angle. Hold for 2–3 seconds. Control the resistance as you return to the starting position.

6. Repeat 5–15 times. Don't let your palms turn up as you pull back, as this can ignite the biceps. Likewise, if palms turn down, the triceps will engage. We want the focus to be on your back muscles, so keep your palms facing each other.

> "*Take a photo of your blocks before stitching them together to keep track of fabric placement.*" —**Sarah Ashford**

Chest

DOORWAY CHEST STRETCH

Place your forearms against a doorframe and take a half-step forward. Feel the stretch across your chest; don't go too far right away; you will progress over time.

ASSISTED CHEST STRETCH

1. Stand tall, holding a measuring tape, therapy band, or towel with both hands behind your back.

2. Use it to gently pull your shoulders down and back slightly.

3. Squeeze your shoulder blades down and together to maximize the stretch.

4. Hold this position for 20–30 seconds, rest, and repeat.

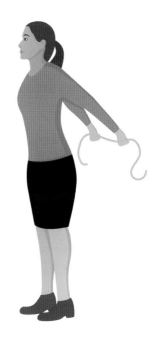

" *Look after your machine as well as yourself! Clean underneath the needle plate after every 10 hours of sewing, and have your machine serviced regularly. Ensure your sewing table is strong enough to support your machine.*" —Jenna Clements

Golfer's Lift

When I need to retrieve a runaway bobbin, I don't bend, I use the *golfer's lift*. Bending creates a C-shape in your spine, whereas hinging from the hips keeps it straighter.

1. While one hand is reaching down to do the lifting, use the other one for stability and balance.

2. As you hinge forward, shift your weight to one leg and lift your other leg behind you as a counterbalance. Keeping your core tight will further protect your spine.

3. Pick the item up and *slowly* return to standing while maintaining a neutral spine. If possible, keep your head above your heart. The important thing is to hinge at the hips without bending your back.

> "*The golfer's lift preserves the 'sweet spot' and the pain-free spine. Hold a chair or other sturdy object with the non-reaching hand; this is great to use in the morning when your spine is at its most vulnerable.*"
> —Dr. Stuart McGill

Torso Stretch

This stretch can be done standing or sitting. If you are seated, place a hand on your knee or a chair, as you stretch toward that side.

1. Sit up straight and reach your left arm over your head, arching your body and allowing your head to relax to the right.

2. Reach up as you stretch the left side of your body open.

3. Take a few deep breaths in this position.

4. As you breathe, your rib cage expands and this encourages a stretch of the muscles between the ribs known as the intercostal muscle. These muscles are important to longarmers who often strain to reach over their frames.

5. Hold for 20–60 seconds and repeat on the other side.

A mechanic's retractable extension magnet can be found in the automotive section of your local hardware store. Use it to pick up your stray pins without bending at all!

Hip Flexors

Your hip flexors shorten as you sit, and quilters sit a lot. Tight hip flexors (the psoas muscles) can really affect your posture, contribute to lower back pain, and give the appearance of a paunch to a flat tummy. This move also provides a lesser stretch to the quadriceps muscles running down the front of your thigh.

1. Before you begin, lock your chair's wheels or stabilize the chair against a wall. To help keep your back straight, activate your core by pulling your belly button in toward your spine.

2. Place your left knee on the chair. Depending on the chair's height, you may need to add a cushion under your knee to keep your hips even.

3. Keep your right leg straight, but don't lock your knee.

4. Squeeze the muscles of your left butt cheek—the side that is kneeling. Feel the front of your left hip lengthen.

5. Hold for 20–60 seconds, switch sides, and repeat.

" *For precision piecing, use an 80-weight cottonized polyester thread, like DecoBob, and a stitch length of 1.6″–1.8″; you'll have very precise seams that lie perfectly flat; your curves will be much smoother.*" —**Bernadette Kent**

Quadriceps

1. Hold onto a chair to help with balance.

2. Bend your left knee back while grasping your ankle with your left hand.

3. Try to line your knees up side by side.

4. Keep your supporting leg straight; do not lock your knee.

5. Concentrate on pushing your shoelaces down into your hand, not on pulling your foot up.

6. Hold for 20–30 seconds, relax, and repeat with the opposite leg.

If you have knee pain or if reaching around to grab your foot is not possible, then modify this move by placing your foot flat on a chair directly behind you.

A sofa works well as you can hold the arm for balance; bare or stocking feet work well on padded furniture.

Keep your shoes on to prevent your foot from sliding across the smoother surface of a wooden chair.

" *Use your hands to keep the area of the quilt between you and the needle flat to avoid puckers when quilting with your walking foot.*" —**Melissa Marginet**

Hamstrings

1. Sit up straight at the edge of your chair, with feet flat on the floor.

2. Extend your left leg, pointing your toes toward the ceiling.

3. Keeping your leg straight, hinge forward at the hips until you feel a pull along back of your thigh.

4. Keep your back straight. Don't worry if you can't touch your toes; the reaching is what's important. You can also loop a measuring tape or band around your flexed foot to help with this stretch.

5. Hold for 20–30 seconds, relax, and repeat with the opposite leg.

STANDING VARIATION

It doesn't take much to feel this stretch. Try it the next time your iron has gone cold and you are waiting for it to reheat. Use your ironing board for support.

1. Standing tall, place your right leg in front of your body with foot flexed, heel pushed into the floor, and toes pointed toward the ceiling.

2. Bend your left knee slightly and gently hinge (not bend) forward from your hips.

" *When foundation paper piecing (FPP) use an Add-a-Quarter ruler to get the perfect ¼″ seam every time. When folding the paper, fold over a postcard, to get a nice crisp, straight line.*" —**Sarah Ashford**

3. Keep your head above your heart and your spine neutral. Hold for 20–30 seconds. Repeat with the opposite leg.

SEW HEALTHY & HAPPY

Hips and Glutes

This stretch helps open the hips and stretches the group of muscles in your hips and glutes.

1. While seated, cross your right ankle over your left knee and sit up nice and tall.

2. Gently hinge forward, keeping your back straight and reaching out with your torso until you feel a stretch in your right glute and hip.

3. Keep your foot on top flexed to protect your knee.

4. Gently press on your right knee to deepen the stretch.

5. Hold for 30 seconds and repeat on the other side.

> " *Use a Hera Marker* and ruler to mark quilting lines on your quilt.*"
> —Sarah Ashford
>
> ** A small tool with a sharp edge that leaves a temporary crease. Marks are visible on both sides of the fabric with no residue.*

Calves and Achilles Tendon

CALF STRETCH

1. Stand with your feet hip-width apart; you can use a chair or wall for support.

2. Step one leg behind, keep your toes forward.

3. Bend your front leg, keeping your back heel firmly pressed down as you lean forward.

4. Hold 30 seconds, rest, and repeat with the opposite leg.

HEEL DROP

1. Stand with the balls of your feet on the edge of a stair.

2. Hold the hand rail to help maintain your balance.

3. Slowly let your heels hang down off the stair until you feel a stretch in the back of your calves and/or Achilles area.

4. Hold for 20–40 seconds, rest, and repeat.

" *You can use all sorts of colours together as long as you keep them all the same approximate tone (amount of grey mixed with pure hue). Avoid mixing fresh, bold prints with muted, grungy ones, and your quilt colour palette will be more harmonious.*"
—Jo Avery

For a seated option, loop a strap or towel around the ball of your foot, then straighten your leg. Slowly tighten the strap. Hold 40 seconds.

Happy Feet

Your indoor shoes might look brand new on the outside but might be worn out on the inside. If your arches are getting sore or you feel the heel cushioning thinning, it's time for a new pair of shoes. Find ones with a low to moderate heel, thick soles, good arch support, and extra cushioning.

Try the following exercises with bare feet.

TOWEL CURL

Grip towel with toes and curl it toward you. Increase resistance by adding weight to towel end.

TOE TAPS

Wiggle toes to loosen them and get blood flowing. Set feet flat on floor and lift each toe one by one, making toes stronger and more flexible.

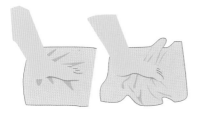

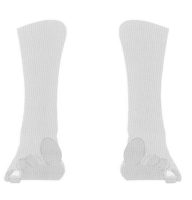

FOOT FLEX

Flexing your foot helps ankle mobility, stretches front of shin when toes are pointed down, and stretches calf when toes are pointed up.

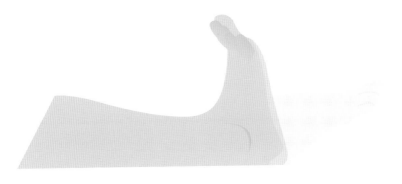

PLANTAR FASCIITIS STRETCH

Sitting on chair with one leg crossed over knee, use hand to gently pull toes of uplifted foot back toward shin of leg.

TOE GRIP

Save your back when you drop something by gripping it with toes and passing it to your hand. Good for your feet, spine, and balance.

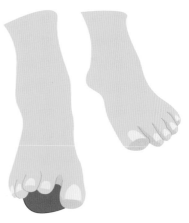

FOOT ROLL

Place foot on a ball and move it back and forth, pressing down as hard as tolerated. Experiment with various sizes and firmness. Frozen water bottle can provide instant relief for tired tootsies.

Healthy Habits

Eat

Michael Pollen summed it up as, "Eat food, not too much, mostly plants." He means real food like vegetables, fruits, whole grains, fish, and meat, and to avoid edible foodlike substances. Practice *hara hachi bun me*, like the Okinawans in Japan, and eat only until 80 percent full.

Change Your Oil

Aside from lubricating your joints and other health benefits, healthy fats are responsible for feeding the brain, protecting your heart, and smoothing those fine lines. Different foods have different essential fatty acids in varying amounts, so eat a variety to stay pain-free.

• Eat nutrient-dense foods. Go for foods that have a variety of vitamins, minerals, protein, and fat packed in one place. Don't waste your time on a cracker when an olive, hard-boiled egg, or a few nuts can feed your brain and keep you young! Juice some greens, and you can drink your veggies while you are pressing those blocks.

• The avocado is natures beauty food. Avocados are naturally sugar-, sodium-, and cholesterol-free. One-third of a medium avocado has twenty vitamins and minerals and 80 calories, which makes it a great nutrient-dense food choice.

• Wild salmon is yummy, but so are sardines, anchovies, mackerel, herring, and trout. A can of salmon in the house means you always have lunch. All are great at fighting inflammation and rebuilding our bodies.

• If you need something fast, two or three olives will go farther than a celery stick. The healthy fat satiates and will keep you fuller longer. If they're looking like they've been around too long, mash them up, call it tapenade.

• Purchase nuts and seeds in smaller quantities and store them in the freezer to prevent rancidity.

> " *I take a multivitamin every day ... it's called an egg!*" —Rosalie Brown

Move

Motion is lotion. Researchers now know that a trip to the gym a few times a week or an evening stroll is not enough to make up for the time spent sitting. We need to move more often, even if it's just for a minute. Every time we get up to walk to the ironing board, dance to some tunes, or do calf raises while we brush our teeth helps! We need to move!

- Aim for at least 150 minutes of moderate-intensity aerobic physical activity throughout the week. That's 30 minutes, 5 times a week. Getting outside has the added benefit of improving mood and helping with sleep.

- Muscle knows no age. If you want to stand taller, live longer, and live independently into your nineties, lift weights! For free low-impact online workout videos and healthy recipes, follow the healthiest grandma I know—Rosalie Brown (page 74)!

- Water has healing properties and exercising in water is easy on the joints. Aqua fit classes are noncompetitive, and no one can see if you mess up a move when you're in the water.

- A good yoga class should leave you feeling loose and calm, not stiff and sore. Try not to overdo it and don't worry about how you look or what your neighbor is doing. "True Yoga" is for all ages, shapes, and fitness levels.

Practice NEAT

Non-exercise activity thermogenesis (NEAT) is the energy you use for everything that is not sleeping, eating, or exercising. Standing is one form of NEAT that can help increase your daily energy output, as is fidgeting, cooking, gardening, typing, or playing with the little ones in your life.

" Workout like your life depends on it, because it does!" —**Rosalie Brown**

Drink

- Drink before you feel thirsty. Have a big glass of water before you start to sew; soon you'll have a reason to get up and walk to the bathroom. When you feel hungry, drink first; thirst is often mistaken for hunger. Drink extra in warm weather and when you are exercising.

- Alcohol, coffee, tea, soda, and energy drinks can all have diuretic effects on the body. Even low levels of dehydration can cause headaches, lethargy, and constipation. Our joints crave hydration—drink up!

- You don't have to drink all your fluids; you can eat them too. Soup, applesauce, and yogurt all provide hydration. Many fruits and vegetables also have high water content, including watermelon, cucumbers, cantaloupe, oranges, lettuce, celery, zucchini, and eggplant. (Visit my blog, page 80, for more info.)

Breathe

Let's not forget about the refreshing benefits of meditation. If meditating is not for you, just close your eyes for 5–10 minutes. No TV, podcasts, or audio books. Just silence or a little music. Elevating your feet during quiet time literally takes a lot of the day's pressure off and boosts circulation.

Sleep

No screens before bed. Bedroom dark and cool. You've heard it all before. There are as many theories regarding the perfect night's sleep as there are quilts that we can't wait to make. The important thing is to go to bed! Ideally on the same day that it is.

"Keep the elastic in your sewing basket. Zippered pants alert us to watch our portions before we eat too much or be prepared to walk it off."
—Pat Skibinski *(Climbed Machu Picchu at the age of 65!)*

Simple Smoothies

A balanced meal has …

… **protein** to build and repair muscle and create new cells.

… **carbohydrates** to give you energy to quilt all day.

… **healthy fat** to fill you up and feed your brain and skin.

So does a smoothie! Smoothies are a quick, balanced lunch or breakfast, with no dishes.

RECIPE Basic Smoothie

The simplest recipe for a quick, nutrient-dense smoothie includes protein, carbohydrates, and healthy fat..

1 scoop protein powder

⅓ cup blueberries

1 tablespoon flaxseed oil or other healthy fat

Add water, ice, and blend. Done!

BUILD YOUR OWN SMOOTHIE

PROTEIN: Protein powders are a convenient way to get your protein in, but there are lots of other options:

• *Dairy:* Options include whey powder, milk, kefir, Greek yogurt, and cottage cheese.

• *Nuts and seeds:* Pumpkin protein powder; chia seeds; hemp hearts; peanut and almond butter; sprouted seeds, such as alfalfa and sunflower—all are high in protein and crammed with micronutrients.

• *Beans:* Soy milk or soft tofu work anywhere; black beans can't be tasted with chocolate; and cannellini beans are great with a vanilla-flavored protein powder.

• *Greens:* Protein powders made from greens add micronutrients in addition to protein, and many vegetables contain protein; try kale, spinach, and watercress.

CARBOHYDRATES: While berries rule, try adding spinach and other vegetables, small amounts of fruit, and powdered greens.

HEALTHY FATS: Flax, chia, and hemp seeds; avocado; coconut water; almond milk

OPTIONAL EXTRAS:

• *Bee pollen:* For immunity

• *Seeds:* For fiber

• *Turmeric:* To fight inflammation

• *What's your favorite extra?*

Quick, Nutrient-Dense Snacks with Rosalie Brown

RECIPE No-Sugar, No-Grain, Peanut Butter Banana Muffins

Easy to make. Freezes well if making ahead of time.

2 ripe bananas

2 eggs

1 cup peanut butter

½ cup plain Greek or Icelandic yogurt

4–6 packages stevia or natural sweetener of your choice

2 teaspoons vanilla

½ teaspoon baking soda

Optional extras:

½ cup hemp seeds

½ cup of sunflower seeds

½ cup chopped walnuts

½ cup dark chocolate chips

1. Mix it all together.

2. Scoop into nonstick muffin tins.

3. Bake at 400° for 12 minutes.

Let cool before eating!

RECIPE No-Bake Protein Balls

Easy and fun to make!

2 cups natural crunchy peanut butter

2 bananas

2 scoops of protein powder (I like vanilla flavored.)

Then get creative! Try adding:

¼ cup sunflower seeds

¼ cup hemp hearts

¼ cup coconut flakes

A bit of grated dark chocolate

1. Mix it all together.

2. Form into quarter-size balls.

3. Freeze for 2 hours on a flat tray.

4. Remove from the tray, place the balls in a resealable bag or container for easy access, return to the freezer or keep refrigerated.

" *Your 50s can feel like your 30s or your 70s ... it all depends on how you live your life!*" —Rosalie Brown

" *If a project becomes too frustrating, it can help to step away or work on a 'no-brainer' project for a break. Sometimes you're too close to the problem to fix it. Make tea, go for a walk, and come back to it later.*"
—Kirsten Smith

Avocados: Good for the Body

When avocados get soft, you have four choices: make a natural mask for your face, spread them on your toast, whip up a salad dressing, or make some yummy guacamole. Goodbye wrinkles and so long muffin top!

RECIPE Avocado Face Mask

The natural oils penetrate the skin to nourish and hydrate. They are packed with vitamin A, fatty acids, and antioxidants that repair the damage caused by the dry air in our homes and pollution.

1 ripe avocado, halved, pitted, and peeled

1 tablespoon honey

1. Mash the avocado into a paste.

2. Mix in the honey.

Apply the mixture to your face. Leave it on for 20 minutes or until it dries completely. Rinse your face with cold water.

You can make this ahead and chill.

RECIPE Avocado Toast

For a single serving.

½ ripe avocado, pitted and peeled

Mash and spread the avocado over the toast. (Leftover guacamole works too.) Top with a fried egg for a breakfast. It will keep you full for hours. For a quick appetizer, try adding bacon, onions, tomatoes, shredded cheese, and balsamic glaze, and then broil. Fancy schmancy!

RECIPE Avocado Dressing

Avocado dressing or even a few slices are a great way to make a salad more satisfying and satiating.

1 ripe avocado, halved, pitted, and peeled

¼ cup water

¼ cup olive oil or plain yogurt

½ or 1 lime, juiced

½ cup cilantro leaves

1 garlic clove, minced

Salt and pepper, to taste

> " *Authentic beauty and joy are connected. It's an inside job.* " —**Pat Skibinski**

Mix ingredients in a blender until combined.

RECIPE Guacamole

2 ripe avocados, halved, pitted, and peeled

1 small onion, finely chopped

1 clove garlic, minced

1 ripe tomato, chopped

1 lime, juiced, salt and pepper, to taste

Mash the avocado to your desired consistency. Stir all ingredients together.

Tip / *Keep the pit in the guacamole or with any unused portions to keep it from going dark.*

Share #quiltersgottaeat—post a picture of the go-to snacks and favorite recipes you like to have on hand to nourish yourself when you're quilting!

Workshop Dos and Don'ts

Workshops, retreats, and charity sewing bees are a great way to learn new skills and enjoy time with quilty friends. Organizers need to find locations that are affordable and available.

Permanent retreat locations cost more because they are better equipped. They should be well lit and equipped with raised cutting tables and adjustable chairs.

FOR YOURSELF:

- *Do* invest in a wheeled travel bag for your machine.

- *Do* bring a thick, firm cushion to raise your chair.

- *Don't* bring your own iron and mini ironing mat.

- *Don't* bring your own mini cutting mat.

Your organizer will supply the necessities. Leave a few of your own things at home so you have to get up, move, and mingle!

" Invest in a sturdy trolley for transporting your machine to classes, it'll be much better for you than carrying it." —Jenna Clements

" When heading off to a retreat, pack many smaller bags instead of a couple of big ones; it's better to make more trips than risking injury, or worse, a chipped ruler!" —Krista Hennebury

" Consider investing in (or borrowing) an inexpensive rolling cart or collapsible wagon to help move your supplies more efficiently." —Krista Hennebury

THE PROS BEHIND THE TIPS

Photo courtesy of Sarah Ashford

Photo by Johnathon Avery

SARAH ASHFORD can be found designing and making quilts, writing, teaching, hosting the *Great British Quilter* podcast, and making glitter project pouches for her Etsy shop. Sarah's GBQ fabric collection Back to Basics is with Dashwood Studio.
@sarahashfordstudio
sarahashfordstudio.com

JO AVERY Quilt and embroidery designer, author, and teacher, Jo loves inspiring others with her colorful designs. When she is not organizing sewing retreats, she can be found designing and producing delightful new patterns inspired by nature.
@joaverystitch
stitchgathering.co.uk

Photo by Rob Brown

ROSALIE BROWN is a world-renowned personal trainer, TV fitness expert, wife, mom, grandmother, and author. She appears regularly on *QVC*, U.S./Europe, and Canada's *Today's Shopping Choice*. Her mission is to help people add more #fungevity to their lives through exercise. *@rosaliebrownfit* • *rosaliebrown.ca*

Photo by Jenna Clements

Photo courtesy of Missouri Star Quilt Company

JENNA CLEMENTS owns Exeter Sewing Machine Company with her husband, Chris, where she teaches sewing by day and quilts by night! She enjoys sharing her passion for quilting and firmly believes that sewing is good for the soul. *@littlejennawren* *exetersewing.co.uk*

JENNY DOAN is a wife, mother, quilter, and the face of Missouri Star Quilt Company. Making quilting simpler is what she is all about. Precuts are the building blocks of her tutorials and quilting designs because they make quilting quick and easy! *@missouriquiltco* *missouriquiltco.com*

> " One more thing ... never eat Cheetos while quilting, unless you have orange fabric!"
> —Jenny Doan

Photo courtesy of Zen Chic

BRIGITTE HEITLAND started sewing when her "feet could reach the pedal," next came interior and textile design, motherhood, an online shop, her book, *Zen Chic Inspired—A Guide for the Modern Quilter,* and her own fabric line with Moda Fabrics. *@zenchicmoda* *brigitteheitland.de*

Photo by Luiza Matysiak

Photo by Rachel Whiting

KRISTA HENNEBURY, a.k.a. Poppyprint, is an international teacher, pattern designer, experienced retreat host, and improv quilting enthusiast. Her modern patterns and her book *Make It, Take It* can be found through Esty and her website. *@poppyprint poppyprintcreates.blogspot.com*

STUART HILLARD is an author, quilt designer, chef, Handi Quilter and AccuQuilt ambassador, and star of the *Great British Sewing Bee*. *@stuarthillardsews stuarthillardmakes.com*

Photo by Tamara Kelly

Photo by Bernadette Kent

TAMARA KELLY is the mastermind behind her website dedicated to crochet, crafts, and world domination. When not having fun with her family, she's busy as a pattern designer, author, presenter, and teacher. *@mooglyblog • mooglyblog.com*

BERNADETTE KENT is a thread educator for WonderFil Specialty Threads. What began as sewing for her kids led to teaching every aspect of quilting, owning a quilt shop, and authoring *Rubies, Diamonds and Garnets, Too*. *@tpastimes twicearoundtheblock.ca*

Photo by Michele ApSimon

Photo by Nicole Marginet

ISOBEL KING (1931–2020) was an award-winning quilter and member of the Guelph GoGo Grandmothers, who raise money for the Stephen Lewis Foundation to support African grandmothers raising their orphaned grandchildren.

MELISSA MARGINET is an avid quilter with a passion for teaching her techniques near and far and empowering quilters to quilt their own quilts at home. She is the author of *Walking Foot Quilting Designs*. *@melissamarginet melissamarginet.ca*

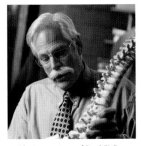

Photo courtesy of BackFitPro

Photo courtesy of AccuQuilt

DR. STUART MCGILL is a professor emeritus of the University of Waterloo, Canada; and author of *Back Mechanic*, which has helped thousands to break bad habits and live pain-free. He is the chief scientific officer for BackFitPro. *@backfitpro • backfitpro.com*

STEVE NABITY As AccuQuilt's CEO (chief energizing officer) and inventor, Steve equates business to coaching. Often overheard asking, "Where's the puck?", or proclaiming, "Go west!," he is blessed with a great team and customers who challenge them to be the best. *@accuquilt accuquilt.com*

Photo by Chet Skibinski

Photo by Kirsten Smith

PAT SKIBINSKI is a Yogafit and WaterART fitness instructor and master trainer with Canfitpro. After retiring from teaching, she began her second career as a flight attendant, which she still enjoys at age seventy. She is also a CPR / first aid trainer with Heart & Stroke and Canfitpro. *facebook.com/1fitbug*

KIRSTEN SMITH is the self-taught crafter behind Barrie-Homemade. As a stay-at-home mom of two energetic boys and active member in the Barrie sewing club, she loves all crafts, baking, and sewing, and is best known for her miniature crochet and sock monkeys. *@barriehomemade* *barriehomemade.ca*

Photo by Christa Watson

Photo by Suzy Williams

CHRISTA WATSON is an award-winning domestic machine quilter from Las Vegas, Nevada, who loves teaching others to find joy in quilting. She designs fabric for Benartex and writes and lectures about her favorite topic—machine quilting! *@christaquilts* *christaquilts.com*

SUZY WILLIAMS is a proud mom, Bernina Ambassador, Bluprint instructor, member of the MQG, and author. With a BFA in visual communications, she uses her graphic design background to transform conventional sewing into her interpretation of minimal, modern design. *@suzyquilts • suzyquilts.com*

AccuQuilt
accuquilt.com

Aurifil Threads
aurifil.com

Bloc Loc Rulers
blocloc.com

Rosalie Brown,
Fitness Professional
rosaliebrown.ca

Edith Choinière, Designer
collectioninedith.com

Fiskars
fiskars.com/en-us

Handi Quilter
handiquilter.com

The Lap App Store
lapappstore.net

Martelli Enterprises
martellinotions.com

OLFA
olfa.com

OttLite Technologies
ottlite.com

United States Dept.
of Labor, Occupational
Safety and Health
Administration:

- *Computer Workstations
  eTool*
  osha.gov/SLTC/etools/
  computerworkstations

- *Sewing*
  osha.gov/SLTC/etools/
  sewing

WonderFil Specialty
Threads
wonderfil.ca

BOOKS

Stay up to date on my tipster's newest book releases on my blog (page 80).

Avery, Jo. *New Patchwork & Quilting Basics*. Lafayette, CA: Stash Books, 2020.

Burns, Eleanor. *GO! Outside the Box*. San Marcos, CA: Quilt in a Day, Inc., 2019.

Doan, Jenny. *Quilter's Precut Companion*. Lafayette, CA: C&T Publishing, Inc., 2015.

Heitland, Brigitte. *Zen Chic Inspired*. Bothell, WA: That Patchwork Place, 2017.

Hennebury, Krista. *Make It, Take It*. Bothell, WA: That Patchwork Place, 2015.

Hillard, Stuart. *Simple Shapes, Stunning Quilts*. New York: Rizzoli, 2019.

Hillard, Stuart. *Use Scraps, Sew Blocks, Make 100 Quilts*. London: Pavilion, 2018.

Kelly, Tamara. *Quick Crochet for the Home*. Fort Collins, CO: Interweave, 2016.

Kent, Bernadette. *Rubies, Diamonds and Garnets, Too*. Lafayette, CA: C&T Publishing, Inc. / Kansas City Star Quilts, 2014.

Marginet, Melissa. *Edge-to-Edge Walking Foot Quilting Designs*. Self-published. 2019.

Marginet, Melissa. *Walking Foot Quilting Designs*. Self-published. 2016.

McGill, Stuart. *Back Mechanic*. (Book plus streamed videos.) Backfitpro Inc., 2015.

McGill, Stuart. *Low Back Disorders*. Champaign, IL, Human Kinetics , Inc., 2015.

McGill, Stuart. *Ultimate Back Fitness and Performance, 6th Edition*. Self-published. 2017.

Pollan, Michael. *In Defense of Food*. New York: Penguin Press, 2008.

Walters, Angela, and Christa Watson. *The Ultimate Guide to Machine Quilting*. Bothell, WA: That Patchwork Place, 2016

Watson, Christa. *Machine Quilting with Style*. Bothell, WA: That Patchwork Place, 2015.

Watson, Christa. *Piece and Quilt with Precuts*. Bothell, WA: That Patchwork Place, 2017.

ABOUT THE AUTHOR

ROSE PARR lives in Guelph, Ontario, Canada, with her husband, David. Together they survived having four children in three and a half years, who are thankfully now all amazing adults. (Can you say *efficiency expert*?) As a personal trainer specializing in older adults, she has worked with many arthritic individuals and, as a nutritionist, helped them choose foods to

Photo by Jake Parr

feel better. In the corporate world she consulted with organizations to implement office ergonomics, and taught staff to stretch at work. After watching her mother spend more time sewing than moving, Rose has made it her mission to work at staying pain-free while continuing to sew for as long as possible. She has combined her studies in home economics with her certifications in ergonomics, fitness, wellness and nutrition to teach others how to *sew smart*.

Her workshops and lectures are available to guilds and at quilt conferences around the world. She is a member of the Association of Canadian Ergonomists, Canfitpro Fitness Professionals, Canadian Quilters Association, American Quilters Society, and local guilds.

VISIT ROSE ONLINE AND FOLLOW HER ON SOCIAL MEDIA!

Blog: healthyquilting.com   **Instagram:** @healthyquilting
Sign up for free monthly tips!

Facebook: /healthyquiltingwithroseparr

I will always be grateful that my mom, Lula, made the time to teach me to sew when I was very young. She enjoyed sewing, knitting, and hand quilting, which as we know involves a lot of sitting. Over the years, her arthritis worsened and eventually she was forced to stop her favorite pastimes. I learned a lot from my mom; what to do, but also what not to do. I am determined to keep my joints happy regardless of my genetics. My father, Lloyd, was practicing NEAT (page 66) before anyone invented the term. He was a machinist and was always moving and tinkering and knew the most efficient way to do anything. I picked up a trick or two from him as well. My thanks to you both.